The Glory of Love

WORDS AND PAINTINGS SELECTED BY
HELEN EXLEY

≣EXLEY
NEW YORK • WATFORD, UK

... the world was newly crowned
With flowers, when
first we met.

THOMAS HOOD (1799-1845), FROM "THE TIME OF ROSES"

There is nothing holier, in this life of ours, than the first
consciousness of love – the first fluttering of its silken wings.

HENRY WADSWORTH LONGFELLOW (1807-1882)

Every kiss provokes another. Ah, in those earliest days of
love how naturally the kisses spring into life. How closely,
in their abundance, are they pressed one against another;
until lovers would find it as hard to count the kisses
exchanged in an hour, as to count the flowers
in a meadow in May.

MARCEL PROUST (1871-1922), FROM "SWANN'S WAY"

OTHER BOOKS BY EXLEY:

A Token of Love   True Love…
Love a Celebration   The Kiss
Our Love Story   Love Quotations
To my very special Wife   To my very special Husband

For Richard.

Published simultaneously in 1995 by Exley Publications
in Great Britain, and Exley Giftbooks in the USA.

12 11 10 9 8 7 6 5 4 3 2 1

Selection and arrangement © Helen Exley 1995
ISBN 1-85015-534-8

Edited and pictures selected by Helen Exley.
Designed by Pinpoint Design.
Border illustrations by Kay Johns and Angela Kerr.
Picture research by P.A. Goldberg and J.M. Clift / Image Select, London.
Typeset by Delta, Watford.
Printed at Oriental Press, UAE.

Exley Publications Ltd, 16 Chalk Hill, Watford, Herts WD1 4BN, UK.
Exley Giftbooks, 232 Madison Avenue, Suite 1206, NY 10016, USA.

A sunbeam filtering through the blind shed a gentle light on her soft golden hair, on her pure throat, on her tranquil breast…. It seemed to me that I had known her for a long time, and that before her I had known nothing and had not lived…. "And here I am sitting opposite her," I was thinking, "I have met her; I know her. God, what happiness!" I almost leapt from my chair in ecstasy….

IVAN TURGENEV, FROM "FIRST LOVE"

I think the time has come, it really has come for us to do a little courting. Have we ever had time to stand under trees and tell our love? Or to sit down by the sea and make fragrant zones for each other? Do you know the peculiar exquisite scent of a tea-rose?

Do you know how the bud opens — so unlike other roses and how deep red the thorns are and almost purple the leaves?

Wander with me 10 years — will you, darling? Ten years in the sun. It's not long — only 10 springs.

Katherine Mansfield (1888-1923),
from "Letters to John Middleton Murry"

When two souls, which have sought each other for however long in the throng, have finally found each other, when they have seen that they are matched, are in sympathy and compatible, in a word, that they are alike, there is then established for ever between them a union, fiery and pure as they themselves are, a union which begins on earth and continues for ever in heaven. This union is love, true love, such as in truth very few men can conceive of, that love which is a religion, which deifies the loved one, whose life comes from devotion and passion, and for which the greatest sacrifices are the sweetest delights.

VICTOR HUGO (1802-1885), TO ADÈLE FOUCHER

Love isn't decent. Love is glorious and shameless.

ELIZABETH VON ARNIM (1866-1941), FROM "LOVE"

Submit to love and it gives a person joy. It intoxicates, it envelops, it isolates. It creates fragrance in the air, ardour from coldness, it beautifies everything around it.

LEOS JANÁČEK (1854-1928), TO KAMILA STÖSSLOVÁ

The madness of love is the greatest of heaven's blessings.

PLATO (427-347 B.C.), FROM "PHAEDRUS"

To love is the great Amulet that makes this world a garden.

ROBERT LOUIS STEVENSON (1850-1894)

Love always creates, it never destroys. In this lies man's only promise.

LEO BUSCAGLIA, FROM "LOVE"

Yes, it was beginning in each

Yes, it threw waves across our lives

Yes, the pulses were becoming very strong

Yes, the beating became very delicate

Yes, the calling   the arousal

Yes, the arriving   the coming

Yes, there it was for both entire

Yes, we were looking at each other

MURIEL RUKEYSER (1931-1980),
FROM "LOOKING AT EACH OTHER"

I love you without knowing how, or
   when, or from where.
I love you straightforwardly, without
   complexities or pride;
so I love you because I know no other way

than this: where I does not exist, nor you,
so close that your hand on my chest is my
   hand,
so close that your eyes close as I fall
   asleep.

PABLO NERUDA (1904-1973), FROM "SONNET XVII"

[Love is] something like the clouds that were in the sky before the sun came out. You cannot touch the clouds, you know; but you feel the rain and know how glad the flowers and the thirsty earth are to have it after a hot day. You cannot touch love either; but you feel the sweetness that it pours into everything.

ANNIE SULLIVAN (1866-1936)

THE HEART'S FRIEND

Fair is the white star of twilight,
And the sky clearer
At the day's end;
 But she is fairer, and she is dearer,
 She, my heart's friend!

Fair is the white star of twilight,
And the moon roving
To the sky's end;
 But she is fairer, better worth loving,
 She, my heart's friend.

SHOSHONE LOVE SONG

The actual thing – inloveness – requires something like a spark leaping back and forth from one to the other becoming more intense every moment, love building up like voltage in a coil. Here there is no sound of one hand clapping…. One who has never been in love might mistake either infatuation or a mixture of affection and sexual attraction for being in love. But when the "real thing" happens, there is no doubt. A man in the jungle at night, as someone said, may suppose a hyena's growl to be a lion's; but when he hears the lion's growl, he knows damn' well it's a lion. So with the genuine inloveness.

SHELDON VANAUKEN

Who, being loved, is poor?

OSCAR WILDE (1856-1900)

I met in the street
a very poor young man
who was in love.
His hat was old,
his coat worn,
his cloak
was out at the elbows,
the water passed
through his shoes, –
and the stars through
his soul.

VICTOR HUGO (1802-1885)

your slightest look easily will

   unclose me

though i have closed myself as

   fingers,

you open always petal by petal

   myself as Spring opens

(touching skilfully,mysteriously)her

   first rose

E.E. CUMMINGS (1864-1962),
FROM "SOMEWHERE I HAVE NEVER
TRAVELLED, GLADLY BEYOND"

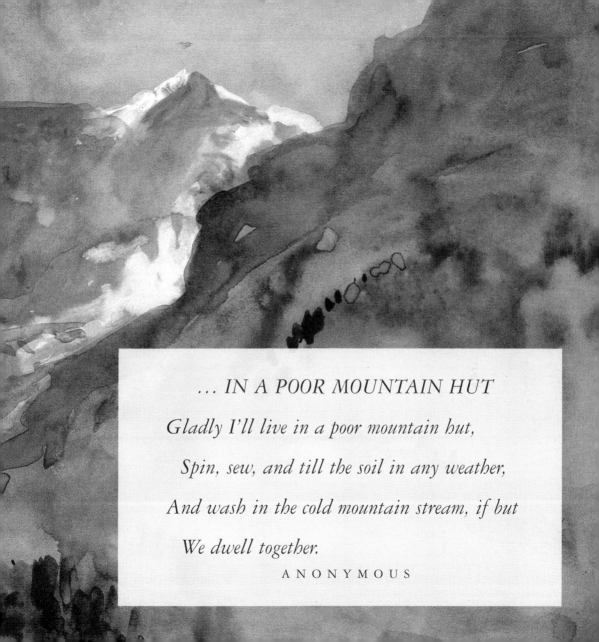

... IN A POOR MOUNTAIN HUT

Gladly I'll live in a poor mountain hut,

Spin, sew, and till the soil in any weather,

And wash in the cold mountain stream, if but

We dwell together.

ANONYMOUS

Peace flows into me

     As the tide to the pool by the shore;
     It is mine forevermore,
It will not ebb like the sea.

I am the pool of blue

     That worships the vivid sky;
     My hopes were heaven-high,
They are all fulfilled in you.

I am the pool of gold

     When sunset burns and dies –
     You are my deepening skies;
Give me your stars to hold.

SARA TEASDALE (1884-1933)

He carried her to the window, so that she too, saw the view. They sank upon their knees, invisible from the road, they hoped, and began to whisper one another's names. Ah! it was worth while; it was the great joy that they had expected, and countless little joys of which they had never dreamt....

Then they spoke of other things – the desultory talk of those who have been fighting to reach one another, and whose reward is to rest quietly in each other's arms.

E.M. FORSTER (1879-1970). FROM "A ROOM WITH A VIEW"

. . .Give all to love;
    Obey thy heart;
    Friends, kindred, days,
    Estate, good fame,
    Plans, credit and the Muse –
    Nothing refuse.

    'Tis a brave master;
    Let it have scope;
    Follow it utterly,
    Hope beyond hope:

    High and more high
    It dives into noon,
    With wing unspent,
    Untold intent;
    But it is a god,
    Knows its own path,
    And the outlets of the sky....

        RALPH WALDO EMERSON (1803-1882)

*Who travels for love finds a thousand miles
not longer than one.*

JAPANESE PROVERB

$\mathcal{L}$ove feels no burden, thinks nothing of trouble, attempts what is above its strength, pleads no excuse of impossibility.... It is therefore able to undertake all things, and it completes many things, and warrants them to take effect, where he who does not love would faint and lie down. Love is watchful and sleeping, slumbereth not. Though weary, it is not tired; though pressed, it is not straitened; though alarmed, it is not confounded; but, as a lively flame and burning torch, it forces its way upwards and securely passes all.

THOMAS À KEMPIS (1379-1471)

It is the true season of Love when we know that we alone can love, that no one could ever have loved before us and that no one will ever Love in the same way after us.

JOHANN WOLFGANG VON GOETHE (1749-1832)

I wonder why love is so often equated with joy when it is everything as well. Devastation, balm, obsession, granting and receiving excessive value, and losing it again. It is recognition, often of what you are not but might be. It sears and it heals. It is beyond pity and above law. It can seem like the truth.

FLORIDA SCOTT-MAXWELL

"I mean that I love you," he said quietly. "You can keep the knowledge, if you care to and it means anything to you. I didn't intend to tell you, but I am told that women like the thought of hopeless love; the more the merrier, perhaps. A little trophy for you, something to hang on your bracelet – like this!" He took off his signet-ring, kissed it and put it into her hand. "When you are an old lady, you can show it to your grandchildren, and say, 'That one was Esmé's – or was it Tom's, or Dick's or Harry's?' Never mind, it will all be forgotten, except that I told you my love when I meant not to, and you had that triumph – meagre as it was against all the others."

She put one palm over the other, the ring safe between them, and wondered what to say. She wanted to clutch at some of his words before they faded, but already they were flying away from her.... "I haven't thanked you. For the ring, I mean, and for what you said.

"No words will come. All I can say is that I love you, too, and have for years and shall for ever."

ELIZABETH TAYLOR (1912-1975), FROM "ANGEL"

PLUCKING THE RUSHES

Green rushes with red shoots,
Long leaves bending to the wind –
You and I in the same boat
Plucking rushes at the Five Lakes.
We started at dawn from the orchid-island:
We rested under the elms till noon.
You and I plucking rushes
Had not plucked a handful when night came!

ANONYMOUS
Translated from the Chinese by Arthur Waley

*W*hen love beckons to you, follow him,
Though his ways are hard and steep.
And when his wings enfold you yield to him,
Though the sword hidden among his pinions
     may wound you.
And when he speaks to you believe in him,
Though his voice may shatter your dreams as
     the north wind lays waste the garden.

For even as love crowns you so shall he crucify
you. Even as he is for your growth so is he for
your pruning.
Even as he ascends to your height and
caresses your tenderest branches that quiver
in the sun,
So shall he descend to your roots and shake
them in their clinging to the earth....

... if in your fear you would seek only love's
peace and love's pleasure,
Then it is better for you that you cover your
nakedness and pass out of love's
threshing-floor,
Into the seasonless world where you shall
laugh, but not all of your laughter, and weep,
but not all of your tears.

KAHLIL GIBRAN (1883-1931), FROM "THE PROPHET"

It seems to me, to myself, that no man was ever before to any woman what you are to me – the fulness must be in proportion, you know, to the vacancy ... and only I know what was behind – the long wilderness without the blossoming rose ... and the capacity for happiness, like a black gaping hole, before this silver flooding. Is it wonderful that I should stand as in a dream, and disbelieve – not you – but my own fate? Was ever anyone taken suddenly from a lampless dungeon and placed upon the pinnacle of a mountain, without the head turning round and the heart turning faint, as mine do?

ELIZABETH BARRETT (1806-1861),
TO ROBERT BROWNING

Love vanquishes time. To lovers, a moment can be eternity, eternity can be the tick of a clock. Across the barriers of time and the ultimate destiny, love persists, for the home of the beloved, absent or present, is always in the mind and heart. Absence does not diminish love.

MARY PARRISH, b.1905, FROM "MCCALLS" MAGAZINE

The need to surrender is one of the great paradoxes of love. Surrender may seem like giving up. Or giving in. But in reality we are strengthened when we actively choose to make ourselves vulnerable. We are empowered by sharing our deepest self with another person, offering him or her our heart, our soul, our life. Surrender is an act of free will. A sacred trust.

ELLEN SUE STERN

I am writing to you, my pen dipped in the pine scent of this afternoon, so that you can breathe the words in and find the image I have for you in my heart. The letters swim in the Adriatic turquoise and clear midsummer skies. There are islands between the paragraphs. Islands of green trees frothing out from bleached rock. Further still await the satin mountains. Feel the caress of their mystical invitation. I am writing to you, while fish leap between the commas and fullstops; iridescent and curved like miniature sunbeams. I hold a stone, a warm pulse in my hand that contains the sun. It is time itself, your time, my time. I parcel it to you, inscribed with memories that flow into deeper hues with each breath.

STEPHANIE JUNE SORRELL, b. 1956

I want my rapscallionly fellow vagabond.

I want my dark lady. I want my angel –

I want my tempter. I want

my Freia with her apples. I want the lighter of

my seven lamps of beauty, honour, laughter,

music, love, life and immortality … I want

my inspiration, my folly, my happiness,

my divinity, my madness, my selfishness,

my final sanity and sanctification,

my transfiguration, my purification,

my light across the sea,

my palm across the desert,

my garden of lovely flowers,

my million nameless joys,

my day's wage,

my night's dream,

my darling and

my star….

GEORGE BERNARD SHAW (1856-1950), TO BEATRICE CAMPBELL

... In our life there is a
single color,
as on an artist's palette,
which provides the
meaning of life and art.
It is the color of love.

MARC CHAGALL, FROM "NEWSWEEK", APRIL 8, 1985

The truth [is] that there is only
one terminal dignity – love. And
the story of a love is not important – what
is important is that one is capable of love.
It is perhaps the only glimpse we are
permitted of eternity.

HELEN HAYES

... You came, and the sun
came after,
And the green grew golden
above;
And the flag-flowers lightened
with laughter,
And the meadow-sweet
shook with love.

ALGERNON CHARLES SWINBURNE (1837-1909),
FROM "AN INTERLUDE"

Here we are
running with the weeds
colors exaggerated
pistils wild
embarrassing the calm family flowers Oh
here we are
flourishing for the field
and the name of the place
is Love

LUCILLE CLIFTON, b.1936, "FLOWERS"

A life without love in it is like a heap of ashes
upon a deserted hearth – with the fire dead, the laughter stilled,
and the light extinguished.

FRANK P. TEBBETTS

Of all forms of caution, caution in love is perhaps the
most fatal to true happiness.

BERTRAND RUSSELL (1872-1970)

To cheat oneself out of love is the most terrible deception;
it is an eternal loss for which there is no reparation,
either in time or in eternity.

SÖREN KIERKEGAARD (1813-1855)

Summer Poem

I will bring you flowers
every morning for your breakfast
and you will kiss me
with flowers in your mouth
and you will bring me flowers
every morning when you wake
and look at me with flowers in your eyes

HEATHER HOLDEN

During the fleeting weeks of that single summer, I lived through my first experience of intense love. All the poetry in my nature centred itself with sudden passion upon a single girl. For me she was the sun and moon, the sea, the hills, and the rivers, the cornfields, the hayfields, the plough-lands, and the first stars of nightfall. Everything that is lovely in nature became illumined by the thought of her: the garden at dawn, as I saw it looking down from the nursery window on the Round-beds and the Crescent-bed, populated with cold, diffident flowers: the meadows by the stream, so hushed in the night air, heavy with the scents of honeysuckle hedges and disturbed only by an occasional deep sighing from one of the ruminating cattle, with weighty body of warm flesh recumbent upon wet summer grass.

From the moment I had seen her in the church I could think of nothing else. My whole approach to life was altered. I no longer cared whether I was to be a poet or not a poet, I no longer was concerned with the deeper problems of existence. Unless I could associate what I saw, heard, tasted, smelt, and touched with her I no longer give it attention.

What reason was there for me to heed the waves that broke day and night against the irregular coasts of the world, to exult in the grass that grew day and night upon the broad back of the stationary land, to watch from ancient elbow-bone bridges the flowing away of rivers, to look up at the crafty midnight stars, unless such appearances could be made to serve in some way as poetical settings for this girl of my utter idolatry? It seemed to me then, as indeed it seems to me still, that every inch of her body shone with some mysterious light….

LLEWELYN POWYS (1884-1939), FROM "LOVE AND DEATH"

My eyes want to kiss your face.

I have no power over my eyes.

They just want to kiss your face.

I flow towards you out of my eyes,

a fine heat trembles round your shoulders,

it slowly dissolves your contours

and I am there with you, your mouth

and everywhere around you –

I have no power over my eyes.

SOLVEIG VON SCHOULTZ, b.1907, FROM "THE LOVER"

Amid the gloom and travail of existence
suddenly to behold a beautiful being, and
as instantaneously to feel an
overwhelming conviction that with that
fair form for ever our destiny must be
entwined; that there is no more joy than
in her joy, no sorrow but when she
grieves; that in her sigh of love, in her
smile of fondness, hereafter is all bliss; to
feel our flaunty ambition fade away like
a shrivelled gourd before her vision; to
feel fame a juggle and posterity a lie; and
to be prepared at once, for this great
object, to forfeit and fling away all
former hopes, ties, schemes, views; to
violate in her favour every duty of society;
this is a lover, and this is love.

BENJAMIN DISRAELI (1804-1881), FROM "HENRIETTA TEMPLE"

I am writing to you on Sunday evening, which is the time I like to write to you best, because I feel the quietest and descend the most into my real self, where my love is strongest and deepest. So you know I always have a fancy at such times that our love makes us somehow alone together in the world. We seem to have a deep life together apart from all other people on earth, and which we cannot show, explain or impart to them. At least my affection seems to isolate me in the deepest moments from all others, and it makes me speak with my whole heart and soul to you and you only.

WALTER BAGEHOT (1826-1877), TO ELIZA WILSON, 1858

We are the dupes of myth when we upbraid

Ourselves because we love; for we are made

For loving: all the sweets of living are

For those that love. Be joyful, unafraid!

THE RUBAIYAT OF OMAR KHAYYAM

Perhaps, after all,
romance did not come into one's life
with pomp and blare, like a gay
knight riding down; perhaps it crept
to one's side like an old friend
through quiet ways; perhaps it
revealed itself in seeming prose,
until some sudden shaft of
illumination flung athwart its pages
betrayed the rhythm and the music;
perhaps ... perhaps ... love unfolded
naturally out of a beautiful
friendship, as a golden-hearted rose
slipping from its green sheath.

L. M. MONTGOMERY (1874-1942),
FROM "ANNE OF AVONLEA"

*T*hese were the days of her poetry, and she said to herself – and she said it too to him, her lips against his ear – that he had made the difference in her life between an unlit room and the same room when a lamp is brought in; a beautiful lamp, she whispered, with a silver stem, and its flame the colour of the heart of a rose.

And Christopher's answer was the answer of all young lovers not two days married, and it did seem to them both that they were actually in heaven.

ELIZABETH VON ARNIM (1866-1941), FROM "LOVE"

... I never see beauty without thinking of you or scent happiness without thinking of you. You have fulfilled all my ambition, realized all my hopes, made all my dreams come true.

You have set a crown of roses on my youth and fortified me against the disaster of our days.

DUFF COOPER (1890-1954)

Lovers don't finally meet somewhere. They're in each other all along.

JALALU'DDIN RUMI, FROM "OPEN SECRET"

Though neither of us was aware of the other before we met, there was a kind of mindless certainty humming along beneath our ignorance that insured we would come together. Like two solitary birds flying the great prairies by celestial reckoning, all of these years and lifetimes we have been moving toward one another.

ROBERT JAMES WALLER, b.1939,
FROM "THE BRIDGES OF MADISON COUNTY"

TO HIS LOVE

Shall I compare thee to a summer's day?
Thou art more lovely and more temperate;
Rough winds do shake the darling buds of May,
And summer's lease hath all too short a date:
Sometimes too hot the eye of heaven shines,
And often is his gold complexion dimm'd;
And every fair from fair some time declines,
By chance, or nature's changing course, untrimm'd
But thy eternal summer shall not fade
Nor lose possession of that fair thou ow'st,
Nor shall Death brag thou wand'rest in his shade
When in eternal lines to time thou grow'st.
So long as men can breathe, or eyes can see,
So long lives this, and this gives life to thee.

WILLIAM SHAKESPEARE (1564-1616)

To hold her in my arms against the twilight

and be her comrade for ever – this was all I

wanted so long as my life should last.... And

this, I told myself with a kind of wonder, this

was what love was: this consecration, this

curious uplifting, this sudden inexplicable joy,

and this intolerable pain.

ANONYMOUS

PICTURE CREDITS

Exley Publications is very grateful to the following individuals and organisations for permission to reproduce their pictures. Whilst all reasonable efforts have been made to clear copyright and acknowledge sources and artists, Exley Publications would be happy to hear from any copyright holder who may have been omitted.

T E X T   C R E D I T S

The publishers are grateful for permission to reproduce copyright material. Whilst every effort has been made to trace copyright holders, Exley Publications would be happy to hear from any here not acknowledged.

ANON: "Plucking The Rushes" translated by Arthur Waley from "170 Chinese Poems". Reprinted by permission of Constable & Co. Ltd.

ELIZABETH VON ARNIM: extracts from "Love", published by Virago Press Ltd.

ELIZABETH BARRETT: extract from "The Love Letters Of Robert Browning and Elizabeth Barrett", edited and introduced by V. E. Stack. Published by Century, a division of Random House Ltd., 1987.

LEO BUSCAGLIA: extract from "Love" © Leo F. Buscaglia Inc., 1972. Published by Souvenir Press, 1984 and Charles B. Slack, Inc.

MARC CHAGALL: extract from "Newsweek" April 8th, 1985.

LUCILLE CLIFTON: extract from "Flowers" from "Good Woman", published by BOA Editions, 1987.

DUFF COOPER: extract from "A Durable Fire: The Letters Of Duff and Diana Cooper, edited by Artemis Cooper, © 1983 Artemis Cooper published by HarperCollins Publishers, 1983.

E. E. CUMMINGS: extract from "somewhere i have never travelled,gladly beyond" is reprinted from "Complete Poems 1904-1962" by E. E. Cummings, edited by George J. Firmage, by permission of W. W. Norton & Co. Ltd. © 1931, 1979, 1991 by the Trustees for the E. E. Cummings Trust and George James Firmage.

E. M. FORSTER: extract from "A Room With A View" , published by Edward Arnold.

KAHLIL GIBRAN: extract from "The Prophet". Reprinted by permission of Alfred A.Knopf Inc. © 1923 by Kahlil Gibran and renewed 1951 by Administrators C. T. A. of the Kahlil Gibran Estate and Mary G. Gibran.

HEATHER HOLDEN: "Summer Poem".

VICTOR HUGO: extract from a letter to Adele Foucher, translated by Christine Czechowski, from "Love Letters" © Antonia Fraser, 1976, published by Weidenfeld & Nicolson in 1976 and Penguin Books, 1977.

KATHERINE MANSFIELD: extract from "Letters to John Middleton Murry". Reprinted by permission of The Society Of Authors as the literary representative of The Estate of Katherine Mansfield.

PABLO NERUDA: extract from "Sonnet 17" from "One Hundred Love Sonnets" by Pablo Neruda, translated by Stephen Tapscott, © Pablo Neruda, 1959 and Fundacion Pablo Neruda, © 1986 by the University of Texas Press.

LLEWELYN POWYS: extract from "Love And Death".

MURIEL RUKEYSER: extract from "Looking At Each Other" from "Collected Poems" by Muriel Rukeyser © 1978, McGraw-Hill, N.Y.

GEORGE BERNARD SHAW: extract from a letter to Mrs Patrick Campbell. Reprinted by permission of the Trustees of Mrs Patrick Campbell deceased.

ELLEN SUE STERN: extract from "100 Meditations For Brides" © 1993 Ellen Sue Stern published by Dell Publishing, a division of Bantam Doubleday Dell Publishing Inc.

ELIZABETH TAYLOR: extract from "Angel", published by Virago Press Ltd.

SARA TEASDALE: "Peace" from "Collected Poems" published by Macmillan Publishing Co. Inc., N.Y., 1937.

IVAN TURGENEV: extract from "First Love", translation © Isaiah Berlin 1950, published by Hamish Hamilton.

SHELDON VANAUKEN: extract from "A Severe Mercy", published by Hodder & Stoughton, 1977.